The Flipchart Guide™ to

Customer
Advisory
Boards

Volume 1

Is your company ready?
A guidebook for executives

D1714123

J. Michael Gospe, Jr.
Author of *The Marketing High Ground*

Copyright © 2013 J. Michael Gospe, Jr.
All rights reserved
ISBN – 13: 978-1479388561
ISBN – 10: 1479388564

The Flipchart Guide™ to Customer Advisory Boards

Why flipcharts? A tool of choice for many facilitators is the flipchart. While this may seem old-school in an era of modern technology, the flipchart visual brings everyone together. It offers a shared experience where all participants can see, comment on, and benefit from the key points, creative thoughts, and "aha!" moments captured from the conversation in real time. It's a customer-engaging technique that encourages the discussion to grow in a purposeful direction.

Two volumes of the *Flipchart Guide™ to Customer Advisory Boards* lead you and your team through every step of the CAB process, showing you how to define and set up the right types of customer conversations that will unlock the Rosetta Stone of customer understanding. They offer strategies, agendas, and case studies used by companies that have successfully deployed CABs to enhance their relationships with strategic customers, improve customer loyalty, and sustain a competitive advantage.

Volume 1: Is your company ready?

Written for executive leaders, this guidebook explores CAB strategies and helps readers assess their organizational, operational, and cultural readiness for embracing a CAB.

- Discover if a CAB is appropriate for your company.
- See how executives use CABs to tune their company's strategic direction.
- Learn where CABs fit into the overall "voice of the customer" (VOC) model.
- Study the *Top 10 List* of what all executives need to know about CABs.

Volume 2: How to execute a world-class CAB meeting
Written for CAB managers, this guidebook provides an operations manual for success:

- View the master timeline for producing successful CAB meetings.
- Unlock the criteria for determining which customers to invite and how to invite them.
- Discover how to build an agenda that will engage customers.
- Review tips and tricks for working cross-organizationally to prepare effective content and presentations.
- Know what to expect from a facilitator.
- Learn how to share CAB feedback internally so your organization can take action.

> For more articles and information about CABs, please visit **http://customeradvisoryboards.wordpress.com**.

Also by J. Michael Gospe, Jr.

Marketing Campaign Development – *What marketing executives need to know about architecting global integrated marketing campaigns*

The Marketing High Ground – *The essential playbook for B2B marketing practitioners everywhere*

The Marketing High Ground series
- **Personas:** *A guidebook on how to build a persona*
- **Positioning Statements:** *A guidebook on how to build, critique, and defend a positioning statement*
- **The Message Box:** *A guidebook on how to tell your story with customer-ready messaging*
- **The Role of the Campaign Manager:** *A primer for driving integrated marketing plans*

Websites
- *Marketing Campaign Development*
  http://marketingcampaigndevelopment.wordpress.com

- *The Marketing High Ground*
  http://marketinghighground.wordpress.com

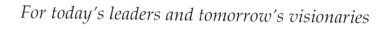

For today's leaders and tomorrow's visionaries

Acknowledgement

Thank you, to all the wonderful people who have generously shared their customer advisory board stories and best practices with me over the past ten years, especially those who have provided me with such expert coaching on this book: Tina Brown, Andrea Davidowitz, Diane Demeester, Sharon Durham, Brian Gentile, Catherine Gibson, Diane Kauffman McGary, Anne Merkert, Sridhar Ramanathan, Susan Thomas, Jeff Tinker, and Melissa Zieger.

I am grateful, too, for the gentle editing from my editors, both of whom are KickStart Alliance co-founders and partners, Mary Gospe and Mary Sullivan. My deep appreciation also goes out to Joe Bednarski for his exceptional work on the cover and figures used in this book.

And most importantly, thank you to my clients, collaborators, and co-conspirators that I have had the honor of working with. Together, we've journeyed to the marketing high ground.

Other types of advisory boards

This book is about customer advisory boards (CABs), sometimes referred to as customer advisory councils (CACs) or executive advisory boards (EABs). But there are also additional types of advisory boards available to business-to-business (B2B) companies, and each serve a unique purpose. These include partner advisory boards (PABs), technology advisory boards (TABs), and influencer advisory boards (IABs).

Companies that sell primarily through distribution channels may be interested in sponsoring a PAB in an effort to improve partner relations and help partners accelerate sales. Companies on the forefront of innovation may be interested in sponsoring a TAB made up of scientists and technologists from the research and development community. The IAB is a new breed, focusing not on the traditional influencers of analysts and journalists, but on individuals whose leadership, innovation, and social interactions inspire others to think differently in how they use technologies, products, and applications.

Although the practical operations of all advisory boards are run in a similar fashion (e.g. facilitated face-to-face meetings held once or twice a year with a carefully selected small group of leaders), there are important differences including the invitee list, specific meeting objectives, and the relevant agendas. Nuances of PABs, TABs, and IABs are not covered in this book; however, the general best practices for establishing an advisory board initiative shared in these pages can be applied to them equally well.

CONTENTS

INTRODUCTION

In 2010, NFI, a leader in trucking, logistics, and warehousing services, hosted its inaugural customer advisory board (CAB) meeting at the Four Seasons in Dallas. Twelve customers, each representing a top tier brand, traveled across the country to attend this robust interactive conversation on the future of their supply chain. When the meeting adjourned, relationships had been strengthened and insights had been gathered that would shape NFI's future roadmap, figuratively and literally. The atmosphere was electric, with conversations buzzing about a renewed sense of partnership and collaboration, with hope and expectations for driving their businesses, and perhaps the larger industry, forward. Now, four years later, NFI's CAB initiative is still going strong. The attending customers continue to give high praise to NFI's leadership team for these valuable sessions, so much so because NFI listens carefully to the input and feedback from its customers and puts it to use.

Customers. How well do you know them? Whoever understands the customer best, wins. In today's highly competitive marketplace, success requires each business-to-business (B2B) company to align with its customers' priorities. So, how well do you know the industry trends, operational issues, and corporate directives driving your customers' businesses? Without this bit of strategic insight, the vision and mission for your company may fail to take root, or a well-intentioned product may turn out to be irrelevant or difficult to sell. A customer-focused market-driven company requires this knowledge. With it, you can reach the *marketing high ground* – that special place where the most capable and competent business leaders reside because they are acknowledged and valued within their company as being customer advocates.

Consequently, it is more important than ever that you hear the "voice of the customer" (VOC) and that you use this knowledge to create competitive solutions that deliver real business value. While a VOC initiative is comprised of a large mix of activities including CABs, customer surveys, polls, interviews, sentiment research, and social media, to name only a few, the focus of this book rests squarely on the strategic value captured within a CAB. A well-run CAB is a highly effective tool for gaining feedback on your company's direction while strengthening relationships with your most important and influential customers. But, what is a CAB?

A CAB is a strategy-level focus group – a sounding board for your leadership team to learn from and better understand your most important customers. This representative group of a dozen customers meets in person once or twice a year to offer advice and perspective on your company direction, value proposition, and product and services suite.

CAB members come together to share perspectives, offer guidance, and explore the intersection of strategic issues affecting their businesses and the value your company can provide to them. During CAB meetings, these customers interact with your company's senior staff who have the authority and responsibility to act on the information gathered.

However, the word "board" can sometimes cause confusion. Is the CAB like a board of directors? Not at all. While a traditional board of directors often provides guidance to an executive team, in its most basic form, a board of directors has a single critical function: to hire and fire the CEO. For a public company, a board of directors has important legal responsibilities. The CAB, on the other hand, has no legal responsibilities, and there is no requirement that any public or private company have a CAB.

In its most effective implementation, a CAB is a cross-functional *initiative*, not an event, and not a single meeting held once or in isolation from the rest of your marketing activities. CAB meetings are unlike any other meeting you will run. They are not sales meetings, nor are they user group sessions offering tutorials or examining product feature details. And, they are not impromptu customer appreciation events where you play golf and socialize. All of those types of interactions are incredibly important and each play a role in the relationship you nurture with your customers. But these are not CABs. It's important to understand the distinction.

CAB initiatives are growing in popularity because they are a very effective tool for validating that your company vision and product direction are in sync with your customers' business plans and priorities.

Executing a world-class CAB initiative requires an unwavering focus on understanding the needs of your customers as well as they themselves do. Equally important is the tight alignment that must exist across the company to ensure execution of a focused business plan and product or services roadmap based, in part, on this very relevant customer input. Unfortunately, the business landscape is littered with companies that refused to take the time to listen to their customers. They thought they didn't need to. The act of listening begins by asking relevant questions of the appropriate leaders in your customer base. But this is just the tip of the iceberg when it comes to the information you need in order to grow your business. Consider that what your customers say they want from you is probably no different from what they tell your competitors. So, what's the point? Where are the opportunities for product or service differentiation?

The most visionary corporate leaders are the ones who not only hear the words spoken by their customers but also read the unspoken needs that lay just below the surface. This type of listening fuels intuition. It's the key to what separates the most innovative companies from a sea of competitors who all have access to the same data but struggle to understand the meaning.

The benefit of customer insight comes from reaching a level of true comprehension of how your customers think as well as behave. And for that, it's critically important to know what questions to ask, and how and when to ask them. For example, all customers want to be pleasantly surprised and delighted, yet it would be counterproductive to ask them directly, *"What can we do to surprise and delight you?"* Either they would respond with superficial, off-the-cuff requests or they wouldn't know how to answer the question. So, you need to find other questions that will provide the level of insight and perspective you need to truly understand the customer. And that requires some finesse.

Written for executive leaders, *Volume 1* offers a guide to assessing your company's organizational, operational, and cultural readiness for a CAB. In these pages, you'll see how executives are using CABs to tune their company's vision and roadmaps. And most importantly, you'll unlock the secrets of how to use the CAB to enhance your relationship with your most strategic customers, improve customer loyalty, and sustain a competitive advantage.

1: IS YOUR COMPANY READY FOR A CAB?

That may seem like a silly question, but customer advisory boards (CABs) are not appropriate for all companies. This is not to imply any judgment, as there are perfectly good reasons for not pursuing a CAB initiative. The CAB is one of the most strategic and important types of customer meeting you will ever run. Think I'm exaggerating? This is the one time, one place where a large portion of your executive staff is in the same room for an extended period of time with a dozen or so of the most influential decision makers in your customer base. Unlike a convention hall or user group setting, this venue is conducive to an intimate conversation about the industry trends, operational issues, and corporate priorities driving your customers' businesses. These are the people who have funded your success and can continue to accelerate your growth or take the wind out of your sales, literally.

Now let's get practical: to understand whether or not a CAB is an appropriate investment, consider these five assessment questions:

1. Are you lacking meaningful, timely, and qualitative customer input?

2. Is your company mature enough for a CAB?
3. Is there executive commitment to support a CAB?
4. Will the leadership team support the CAB as a cross-functional initiative?
5. Is it the right time for a CAB initiative?

Success or failure of a CAB initiative can be linked back to the answers to these questions. If even one of these questions presents a point of organizational, operational, or cultural concern, then a CAB may not be your best option, at least for now.

1. **Are you lacking meaningful, timely, and qualitative customer input?**

Brian runs an open source software company using a business model that puts him in constant communication with his customers. He's established a community of customers and users who provide feedback in a variety of forums, from industry surveys, to "feature voting", to physical as well as virtual "meet ups" where customers, users, and company representatives come together to innovate, dissect trouble spots, and share best practices. In fact, his business is run like a nearly constant CAB. In Brian's case, investing in a traditional CAB initiative would be redundant because he already has an ongoing stream of customer connections.

In contrast, Allison's business doesn't have a constant nor consistent mechanism for gathering customer input and feedback about priorities and strategic direction. Her last customer survey was conducted a year ago, and she knows those answers are now out-of-date and meaningless. In the meantime, any insights about customer growth plans and priorities are harvested from talking individually with her sales or customer support reps. Making sense of this single source of information is more difficult because each sales rep has a different perspective depending on how close they are to making quota. Allison knows she needs to formalize a direct dialog with customers who can provide more reliable and meaningful directional guidance to her leadership team. The CAB is an obvious choice for her company.

2. Is your company mature enough for a CAB?

Ron is a CEO of a startup company. He's grown his business over the past few years and has won an initial set of customers. Speed-to-market is his most important metric, and as such, he's surrounded himself with technology and operational mavericks who work diligently around the clock to win the next order. There is no time to plan further than the next quarter. If asked about the importance of gathering customer input, Ron would respond that he already knows what he needs to do and that whatever customers said wouldn't make any difference. He drives his business to achieve success one customer at a time. Ron's is a common strategy for startups, and to invest in a CAB before he has an established market segment with a critical mass of customer success, and before he's developed a repeatable go-to-market plan, would be premature. However, the lack of a CAB in no way implies that Ron doesn't care about customers and their priorities. He most definitely does. But based on where his company is in its growth cycle, his company is not ready to initiate a CAB.

Gary, on the other hand, is the CEO of a long-established telecommunications company. His company has been running a formal CAB initiative for five years; and he's tasked the marketing organization to lead the ongoing cross-functional effort and execute CAB meetings in the US and

Europe. Based in no small part because of the CAB, many of his customers view his company as a "trusted advisor" and not just a common vendor; the CAB is a proof point that shows customers that he and his team are sincere when they ask customers what they think. He welcomes customer input and perspective to guide future investments. CAB meetings have been both hard-hitting and inspirational. He relies of this group to help keep his company on track.

3. Is there executive commitment to support a CAB?

Frank is a chief marketing officer (CMO) of a growing software company. Coming from a sales background, Frank loves to be in the midst of action, participating with the sales team to close the next set of deals. On the heels of a successful year he became the executive sponsor for a CAB initiative. Because of his hands-on nature and a priority to carefully manage costs, he decided to drive the process and facilitate the meeting himself. Unfortunately, Frank often missed CAB preparation meetings, as other business issues required his attention. On the day of the event, he told his logistics manager that she would have to facilitate the meeting because "something had come up." Horrified, but with a "show must go on" attitude, she walked into the hotel's ornate conference room. There, she spied a dozen senior executives from her most strategic customers sitting quietly around the U-shaped conference table wondering as to the reason for the delay of the start of the meeting. She was a trooper and ran the meeting as best she could. Customers were polite in their participation, but through back channels they voiced their displeasure regarding the novice facilitator and the obvious disappearance of the CMO and CAB sponsor. A wave of severe disappointment washed over these customers as they realized their presence was not as important as they were led to believe. Frank let other business issues distract him from the CAB, and as a result the company's credibility, as well as his own, was significantly damaged. The CAB initiative wobbled then died because of a lack of executive commitment.

Conversely, Bill has been a CAB advocate for the past 10 years. As the CEO of a major technology firm, he invests personal time with his staff to set and review CAB objectives. He's vocal about the imperative to learn from his customers, and he embodies a "customer first" attitude in everything he does. Bill's attitude flows through his leadership team and the logistics managers who run the details of every CAB meeting. And he hired a professional facilitator to guide the planning process and facilitate the CAB to ensure a smooth operation with no hiccups. Bill's attitude is infectious and continues to pay off in dividends with customers eager to return to the CAB again, again and again.

4. **Will the leadership team support the CAB as a cross-functional initiative?**

Amy is a senior VP of a business unit at a computer company, and she believes in the promise of the CAB. Eager to embrace a CAB to help guide her team's priorities, she reached out to experts within and outside her company to explore the possibilities of gathering and synthesizing this type of customer input and perspective. To her surprise, internal audiences responded with significant pushback. Other groups inside the company were not interested in Amy's vision for such an initiative. Their response had less to do with the value of a CAB and everything to do with internal politics. Unfortunately, rather than promoting unity and energizing the wider business strategy, the CAB became a political football with issues around who should lead it. It died due to a lack of cross-functional cooperation.

Jean, however, is a visionary and an advocate for internal synchronization and alignment at her transportation and warehousing company. It was her idea to propose the CAB concept to the leadership team. The CEO was not familiar with the benefits of the CAB and was reluctant to embrace the idea at first. In response, she reached out to specific long-term customers to inquire as to their willingness to participate. The common reaction was, "definitely" and "it's about time!" This immediate and energetic customer response proved instrumental in winning full internal endorsement. She successfully rallied her cross-functional leadership team and the CAB soon became a unifying initiative that reaffirmed and strengthened their relationship with key customers. Now, four years later, the CAB has become part of the company's culture with the executive team taking great pride in being one of the few companies in their industry to embrace a CAB initiative.

5. **Is it the right time for a CAB initiative?**
    Timing is everything. When Steven joined an innovative hi-tech startup as its chief innovation officer he knew he needed more customer input to help the leadership team set and confirm its value proposition. He introduced the CAB concept to the leadership team and received the go-ahead to develop a detailed plan. Unfortunately, two unplanned events crippled the execution of the CAB: a reorganization resulted in the hiring of a new CMO who was not familiar with the value of a CAB initiative; and business conditions required accelerating the launch of a new product. As a result the CAB was pushed down the priority list. All work

associated with CAB preparation was delayed until a week before the event. Poor planning resulted in a lopsided group of invited customers; presentations were tossed together with little thought to the desired dialog with customers. The CAB meeting failed to meet the intended objective. In the end, the attending customers and company executives walked away scratching their heads wondering if the event had been a good use of time. The company would have been better served if they had reaffirmed their CAB strategy and reprioritized it so they had more time to prepare properly.

Jane is the CEO of a fast-growing software-as-a-service (SaaS) company and is a firm believer in CABs, having executed such initiatives at two prior companies. The question, though, was when to hold the first meeting. As she pondered this, the leadership team met at an executive offsite to wrestle with a few strategic questions that would shape the course of her company. They decided to use the CAB as a resource to review, validate, and rank the merits of several potential investment opportunities that arose from the executive offsite. Thus, the timing of the CAB coming six weeks after this critical executive offsite proved beneficial. Relevant issues were identified and explored at the CAB with tangible implications and action items for both the company's short-term roadmap and longer-term investment strategy.

Four CAB Objectives

If you decide to pursue a CAB initiative, there are four primary objectives for each well-run meeting. A company may want to achieve just one, all four, or a combination of these general objectives:

1. **Gain a better understanding of the trends, drivers,**

and priorities shaping your customers' businesses, and to explore how your company can become a more valuable partner in light of these influences.

2. **Validate your company's value proposition and strategic direction**, ensuring your business is in sync with your customers' needs and expectations.

3. **Review, assess, or brainstorm product direction and opportunities**, improving solutions, interaction, and customer satisfaction.

4. **Collaborate on shared business issues**, thereby strengthening the relationship between your executives and customer decision makers, and fostering peer-to-peer networking opportunities between your customers.

If the above objectives mesh with your interests, then a CAB is the right initiative for you. This is a critical first step because CABs are often misunderstood as having other objectives that are *not appropriate*. For example:

x   Do not use the CAB as a sales event to drive immediate bookings. *Instead, host a breakfast meeting for a mix of customers and prospects where customers are invited to talk about specific applications and use cases for your products and services.* (This is worth repeating: **the CAB is not a sales event!** If you attempt to sell to customers during this meeting, they will feel that you tricked them, your brand image will suffer, and they will not return to future CAB meetings.)

x Do not use the CAB merely to socialize with customers. *Instead, add a customer-appreciation day at the end of your annual user conference.*

x Do not use the CAB to prioritize product features or conduct product training. *Instead, hold a product focus group or training event with actual users.* (Decision-makers attend CABs; they may or may not be the actual users of your products or services.)

x Do not use any CAB meeting to publicly launch new products or services. *Instead, execute an integrated marketing campaign to introduce new products and services, taking full advantage of relevant and timely marketing and social media vehicles necessary to engage prospects and customers through their buying cycle.*

x Do not use the CAB to discuss support issues unique to each customer. *Instead, set up a private quarterly (or semi-annual or annual) account review meeting with each customer.*

A CAB Checklist

So, is a CAB initiative right for your company? The following page offers a checklist to help you decide.

Is a CAB initiative right for your company?
10 positive signs

√ The industry is going through significant change (e.g. an economic downturn or recovery, influx of new regulations, entry of new technologies or competition), and customers are rethinking their strategy.

√ As a strategy-level focus group, the CAB is a welcomed complement to our other VOC or customer engagement efforts, including surveys, product focus groups, and user group meetings.

√ We are honestly interested in knowing what customers think.

√ We are willing to take action based on customer input and feedback.

√ We are willing to make a financial and a resource investment to support a CAB initiative.

√ The entire executive staff is onboard and eager to support the CAB initiative.

√ All department heads from marketing, product development, engineering, customer support, and sales are engaged and supportive of the CAB initiative.

√ We are ready to engage customers in a strategic business-focused conversation; we have discussion topics worthy of an agenda.

√ The timing of the CAB fits well with regard to other strategic planning meetings and events that have been (or will be) scheduled.

√ We have a critical mass of customers that we can choose from to invite to our CAB.

Why Your Customers Will Participate in a CAB

Senior decision makers attend CAB meetings for three primary reasons. First, they rarely have the opportunity to network with their peers to discuss and debate how the world around them affects their business. They are eager to explore and compare notes with other executives who are wrestling with the same business challenges. They want to learn from each other.

Second, they want to get a clear picture of your vision and business strategy and explore how they can influence it and take greater advantage of the benefits your company offers. Briefings on product direction, early access to products before general release, hands-on with prototypes, and unprecedented access to your company's leadership team all provide a unique and compelling opportunity to gather and discuss information that can only be obtained under a non-disclosure agreement.

And third, it is very rare to find vendors that are genuinely interested in learning what customers think. Customers have opinions they want to share with their vendors, if only the vendors would ask them sincerely, politely, and with an honest intention to listen and act on their input. So, when a company extends a thoughtful invitation to senior decision makers to come together with their peers and provide guidance and feedback, many customer executives jump at the chance. To confirm these reasons, here is some feedback customers have offered at the close of CAB meetings.

"I feel honored to be invited to participate with this elite group of strategic customers."

"It's about time! I've been waiting for a meeting like this where I can share feedback. Thank you for inviting me."

"I appreciate your spending time on the strategic issues that are important to my business."

"It's not often that I am invited to contribute in an executive roundtable. I very much appreciated the opportunity to offer my input and feedback on your company vision and direction."

"I enjoyed participating in a lot of very interesting discussions and spending time together and exchanging ideas."

Commitment to Your CAB

If you decide to embrace a CAB initiative, you need to be sure you are ready and committed to do what's required to make it a success because you'll only get one chance with this group of elite customer leaders. CABs are not about lectures presented by company brass; they are about discussions that engage customers where everyone learns from each other. Your commitment to the CAB starts by practicing active listening as your customers respond to the topics you put before them.

Active listening is a communication technique that requires the listener to feed back what they hear to the speaker, by way of re-stating or paraphrasing what they have heard in their own words, to confirm what they have heard and moreover, to confirm the understanding of both parties.

Wikipedia

Active listening is about understanding *then* engaging in a dialog in a way that leads to a more productive business outcome than would otherwise be possible. But your commitment doesn't end here. While it is not required that you agree with everything these customers say, and it is not expected that you will take action on every suggestion, it is required that you consider this valuable input in your decision-making process. If you decide to act, or if you decide not to act, customers will want to know why. They'll expect an update at the next CAB meeting. In short, commitment requires your willingness to keep the doors of communication open during and after the meeting.

2: THE CAB AND THE "VOICE OF THE CUSTOMER" MODEL

> *"Voice of the customer" (VOC) is a term used in business and Information Technology to describe the in-depth process of capturing a customer's expectations, preferences and aversions. Specifically, the VOC is a market research technique that produces a detailed set of customer wants and needs, organized into a hierarchical structure, and then prioritized in terms of relative importance and satisfaction with current alternatives.*
>
> Wikipedia

More companies today are making it a priority to update and energize their customer interactions. Yet while recognizing and treating the value of customer input and feedback as a priority is a good thing, allowing each department open reign for their own interaction with customers, out of sync with the interactions being driven by other departments, leads to internal confusion and duplication of resources. And this says nothing of the growing annoyance customers are likely to feel as they are bombarded with multiple uncoordinated requests for information from your company. The secret to harnessing the power of customer input is to ensure that each touch point is part of a comprehensive "voice of the customer" (VOC) model – a model that is shared across the enterprise.

In reality, gathering, sharing, and acting upon customer input and feedback is not a task that lives with a single individual or a specific team. Different departments require different pieces of customer data at different times. Adopting a comprehensive VOC model allows everyone across the enterprise to see the "big picture" and to leverage data that is captured by others, while making their data available to all.

Figure 1: An enterprise "Voice of the Customer" model.

Where Does the CAB Fit?

Setting up a VOC model can be as complex as a Rubik's Cube, with constantly shifting objectives, participants, and questions requiring customer input and feedback. One way to simplify this model is shown in the pyramid graphic illustrated in Figure 1. It centers on the type of customer input enterprise companies are interested in gathering: from tactical and operational (i.e. customers providing real-time feedback on the day-to-day interaction), to product direction (i.e. marketers gathering information that drives the short/mid-term product roadmap), to strategic business direction (i.e. executives exploring value propositions against the industry trends, business drivers, and priorities shaping your customers' businesses).

Investigating each type of customer input requires a different set of tools and best-practices, used by different people, and executed at different times to engage unique subsets of customers. Figure 2 reveals some of the typical activities that are part of the VOC model. CABs are a tool-of-choice used to capture the mid/long-term focus associated with strategic business topics.

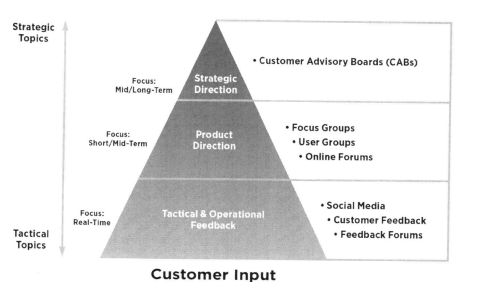

Figure 2: "Voice of the customer" activity sample.

The key to a successful VOC model is the alignment and interaction of every customer touch point so that the entire company benefits from the collected information. Customers will also recognize and appreciate any vendor or partner that treats them with respect when gathering this information. To fully understand how these pieces fit together, we need to break down the organizational silos.

Breaking Down the Silos

Although this may seem obvious, it is surprising that many managers don't actually know or have access to all the customer data that exists within their company. While systems issues may be part of the limitation, a bigger problem is usually the lack of a consistent set of operational processes, techniques, and templates for gathering this data and sharing the results internally. For example: product team A is very effective in conducting focus groups, but product team B is unaware of team A's best practices, so they soldier on by creating their own set of sub-standard tools. Meanwhile, the director of product team A leaves the company taking his undocumented knowledge of focus group best practices with him. There is a smarter way to work. It starts by breaking down the silos.

- **Customer support** organizations are interested in collecting real-time customer feedback on products, services, ordering, fulfillment, bugs, fixes, etc. As such, their universe consists of every customer. Tools they use to collect this input and feedback typically include online or printed surveys, feedback forms, call centers, message boards, and social media.

- **Product management** teams are interested in gathering insight about product use-cases and exploring product directions. A key goal of this team is to understand customer priorities regarding feature sets, user interfaces, and such. Those insights are commonly reflected in a product requirements document (PRD) revealing the tactical and technical details of how, when, and where customers are actually using (or how they want to use) the product. Typical customer interaction points may include product focus groups, user group meetings, and online forums. It's not practical to get in-depth product direction from every customer, so they focus on a smaller subset of identified users. They are typically hosted by a product director and include one or two subject matter experts (SMEs) who can add more details when responding to customer questions.

- **Product marketing** and **solution marketing** teams investigate a broader perspective by focusing on the business problem or objective the customer is trying to solve. These teams are searching for, then aggregating, customer use-case data (as opposed to product use-case data). These *customer use-case focus groups* are different from the *product-based focus groups* hosted by their product management counterparts. Customer use-case focus groups may be conducted blind, where the attendees don't know which company is asking the questions; or they may be company-hosted. They start by spotlighting a premise of a customer problem, issue or objective. In other words, they don't start the meeting with a question about feature X; instead, they establish a problem context first. Hearing customers explain what they are doing or trying to do and how they compare and contrast product alternatives, in their own words, can be eye-opening. Product marketers also tend to be more interested in discovering the relevant value their product provides specific vertical segments. They seek to find answers to why customers purchased their product, and why others didn't. The output of their investigation is typically captured in a market requirements document (MRD).

- **Corporate marketing** teams focus on the company's brand. Often times this group is the steward of the company's vision, mission, and the larger value proposition. They seek to understand more about the industry trends, business drivers, and priorities that are shaping their customers' businesses. The CAB initiative fits here. Whereas product focus groups engage users, and customer use-case focus groups will invite managers and directors, a CAB represents a more intimate dialog with a smaller set of senior executive decision-makers who are responsible for driving their businesses forward. The CAB is also a productive sounding board for your executive staff to test ideas and preview business plans with leaders from your most strategic customers.

- **Sales organizations** don't own the VOC process per se, although they are a huge proxy for the customer voice within your company. Marketing and sales teams must always be tightly aligned. While it is not required that the sales organization approve every marketing tactic, they should never be surprised. With specific regards to the CAB, it is appropriate for sales reps to nominate their customers for CAB membership; however, they do not decide the final membership. The promise of CAB membership should never be a customer perk offered by sales reps as an incentive to close a deal. That sets the wrong expectation on both parties. But it is appropriate for sales reps to follow-up with CAB customers after the meeting. It's a perfect way to further assess their interests and needs. And it presents an opportunity to offer a prescription or recommendation for other products or services the customer may not have yet discovered.

For a CAB initiative to be successful, all employees need to understand and appreciate the VOC model or they risk inviting the wrong customers to answer the wrong questions. CAB meetings do not represent a free-for-all where any and all questions are fair game, yet this misinterpretation is surprisingly common with some executives, especially with those who have never before participated in a CAB. This misunderstanding is the source of much internal frustration that tends to manifest itself in the final weeks prior to the CAB meeting. A warning sign is when team members, days before the meeting, suddenly want to reevaluate the CAB's objective and battle over the attendee list and the agenda. The good news is that this confusion can easily be mitigated when the team takes the time to understand the VOC model and acknowledge how the CAB can be best applied to their company.

Adopting the VOC and CAB as Corporate Initiatives

Chances are your organization is already executing many of these programs and tactics. But how aligned are these efforts? Is the information collected in a way that can be easily shared across the company? And, most importantly, how are company leaders acting on this feedback to make decisions? Investing time and money to gather customer input in a splintered fashion slows your company's ability to innovate because it adds a layer of confusion and creates a political divide between those employees who have access to the data and those who don't.

The answer is not to delegate this responsibility downward but to establish a company mandate requiring marketing, sales, product management, engineering, and customer support to participate together in a VOC model that shares customer feedback so everyone can make the best business decisions possible. This does not happen naturally. Becoming a customer-focused market-driven company requires discipline, commitment, and an agreement to a set of shared company objectives that ensures alignment. Three critical ingredients are necessary to inspire the behaviors you want to encourage:

1. **Constantly reinforce a culture that's open to listening and change**. The members of the executive staff must visibly embody this culture. When the rank and file see how listening to customers is actively shaping internal debates and discussions, it becomes real. If, on the other hand, executives are standoffish, showing little appreciation for listening to customers or referencing customer data to support their recommendations and decisions, then trust and commitment to the VOC model will wane.

2. **Appoint a VOC executive sponsor to lead the cross-functional initiative.** While it is critically important that this be a shared initiative, it still must have an identified leader. Give this leader both the responsibility and the authority for bringing a cross-functional team together to design the most effective VOC model. More importantly,

give the VOC executive sponsor the power to reward teams and individuals appropriately. In fact, contributions to the VOC model must become a component in everyone's annual performance evaluation because what gets measured and rewarded becomes reality. In many companies the VOC executive sponsor and the CAB executive sponsor are the same person, often the CMO or VP of marketing.

3. **Be patient.** Becoming a customer-focused market-driven organization takes time. If you are serious about it, it needs to be engrained in the company's culture. Set a two-year timeframe for the model, with appropriate milestones. It takes longer than a quarter to see and understand the positive implications of your VOC activities. The results won't be obvious at first. Give your employees time to embrace, refine, and own the model.

3: USING THE CAB TO TUNE YOUR STRATEGIC DIRECTION

A CAB is a strategy tool that should tie directly to your annual business planning process. It should not be treated in a vacuum. Here's an example of how one CEO linked the two.

John and his team were working very hard to grow and accelerate the business; yet while everyone was busy, the team members were not aligned with a common set of priorities. When asked individually about the strategic direction of the company, each person gave a different answer and only one individual could crisply articulate the company's vision. In addition, team leaders did not agree on how to measure customer success. Intuitively, the team knew they had to realign their efforts and validate the company's direction against the needs of their customers, but they didn't know how to do that.

That's when John decided to hold an executive offsite to capture a shared vision and drive the alignment of the company's priorities. Afterwards, his team launched a CAB initiative to help them tune and validate the company's strategic direction. In doing so, he successfully linked the formation a CAB to his planning process.

While the executive offsite and the CAB may feel like two independent activities, think of them as two chapters in the same book. The planning exercises set the premise for the plot of your customer story. John's team followed these six steps:

Step 1: Hone the objective of the internal strategy-setting meeting

Executives report that they spend a significant amount of time in meetings that are poorly run and do not produce meaningful results. This is especially true when meetings focus on complex issues. With this in mind, the CEO gave careful thought to three objectives for this executive offsite:

1. Review, refresh, and reaffirm the business strategy.
2. Define guidelines on how the team should execute the business strategy.
3. Capture and prioritize strategic questions requiring customer input and feedback, given the operational implications of these guidelines.

The CEO was also clear on setting expectations on what would *not* be discussed during this meeting, namely:

x   Reviewing operational plans,
x   Discussing tactical details (e.g., should the poster be red or blue?), and
x   Problem solving.

The desired output was specific: alignment among team leaders regarding the business vision, identification of strategic issues that needed immediate attention, and agreement upon a list of questions requiring customer input and feedback that could be explored during the CAB (see step 6).

Step 2: Identify and address the right strategic topics

To promote shared ownership, the CEO invited his staff to *list and describe* the strategic issues they wanted to discuss. He went further by assigning specific topics to the individuals who requested them. Those people then became responsible for framing the conversation on his or her requested topic.

The agenda for this executive offsite included several discussion topics (not presentations). Each topic required one or two slides to set up. Then, it focused on a single question for the team to explore. Discussion topics ran between 30 – 60 minutes. This kept the momentum going without the team feeling like they were debating the same issue over and over again. The following is the agenda the CEO used with his leadership team:

Agenda for a Strategy-setting Offsite

8:30   Opening comments & objectives for the day
8:40   "Visualizing success" exercise (see step 4)
9:15   Operational guidelines discussion
        1. Defining our differentiation: *What primary value do we provide and how do we defend it?*
10:00 BREAK
10:15   Guidelines discussion continued
        2. Market segment prioritization: *Should we actively focus on three segments or only two?*
        3. Market readiness: *How do we ensure our products are ready for market so that customers are satisfied?*
11:45 LUNCH
12:30   Guidelines discussion continued
        4. Competition: *How do we balance our bookings target against competitive pressures?*
        5. Operating under resource constraints: *Are we focused or are we doing too much?*
2:00 BREAK
2:15   Reaffirm corporate vision and growth strategy
2:45   Documenting the output, next steps & action items
3:00 ADJOURN

Step 3: Establish rules of engagement

For meetings to be productive, follow a set of rules. These are quite simple, yet they are frequently ignored.

- Start and end the meeting on time. *Being respectful of the time commitments of others makes it easier for the group to stay focused.*
- Clearly state the objective for the day. *It's surprising*

34

how many meetings start with people talking with no confirmation on why they are attending or what specific end they want to achieve.

- Specify what topics are <u>not</u> allowed. *This avoids wasting time on irrelevant topics.*
- Encourage discussions, not presentations. *Productive time with the executive team is limited; spend it on collaborating, not updating or educating each other.*
- Create an atmosphere of equality. *For individuals to feel empowered, they must be free to speak openly and honestly without fear of retribution.*
- Avoid interruptions by turning off cell phones, laptops, and tablet computers off. *Don't allow distractions and multi-tasking to disrupt the discussion.*

Step 4: Invite creativity by using the "Visualizing Success" exercise

When it comes to business strategy offsites, it's helpful to find out what success means to each participant. Use this exercise as an icebreaker to get their creative juices flowing:

- Break the team into small groups of 2-4 people.
- Premise: Two years from now your company will be on the cover of <u>TIME</u> or <u>Forbes</u> (or magazine of your choice).
- What's the headline? What's on the cover? And, what's the article about?
- Participants have 15 minutes to sketch their cover on a flipchart.
- During the final 20 minutes, each group shares their personal vision of success.

After a moment or two of hesitation, everyone will get

engaged. The short time limit sparks creativity, and the noise level will rise as people become animated in describing their visions of success. The energy is infectious. When conducting this exercise, look for threads of commonality and differences between the teams. It will become immediately clear how aligned the individuals are by the end of this exercise. The rest of the agenda can be tuned to addressing any alignment issues that may require attention. The sketched magazine covers stay up on the wall throughout the meeting. Team members will constantly refer back to them as the agenda unfolds throughout the day. It can be a powerful unifying force.

Step 5: Facilitate the meeting for success

Running a successful strategy offsite yourself isn't always as easy as it sounds, especially when you need to balance managing the meeting while actively participating in it. Consider partnering with a facilitator (either an internal resource or an external professional business facilitator) who can help you do both. A good facilitator will provide the following value:

- Ensure the meeting starts and ends on time,
- Allow equal participation from all team members so one person doesn't dominate the discussion,
- Use flipcharts or other tools to guide and track the conversation, and
- Create a "parking lot" for issues that arise but that aren't appropriate for discussion at this meeting.

In this particular case, the single, most valuable contribution a facilitator makes is in being able to summarize each discussion, distilling the many points into a crisp guideline statement that addresses the strategic topic. When selecting a facilitator, look for someone with these characteristics:

- The ability to navigate the conversation and offer an action-oriented conclusion to each topic,
- Is unbiased and unaffected by internal politics, thus freeing him or her to ask the unspoken questions that the team may be uncomfortable asking, and
- Familiar with your team and your business so he or she can credibly prescribe the obvious (and not-so-obvious) action items and ask for ownership of each action item.

A seasoned facilitator will ensure that the team walks away feeling that the offsite was a good, productive use of their time.

Step 6: Kickstart the CAB planning process

By now you may be wondering what steps 1 – 5 have to do with the CAB. The simple answer is, *everything*! Your vision, operational guidelines, and strategic priorities are meaningless if they don't connect you with your most strategic customers. For each guideline discussed during a strategy-setting meeting like this there are both strategic and operational implications worthy of customer input and feedback. There is a CAB-relevant corollary question for each of the strategic issues discussed. In this example, here were some of the topics explored at John's strategy-setting meeting and how each evolved into a CAB-worthy set of questions:

Guideline #1: Defining our differentiation

Internal question: *What primary value do we provide and how do we defend it?*

CAB variation: *How would you define the value we're providing to you? What kind of business partner do you consider us to be? And, how might we become a more valuable partner to you and your company in light of the trends and drivers affecting your own businesses?*

Why these questions are important: There is a difference between what a company sells and what a customer buys. This is an opportunity for customers to share, in their own words, why they buy from you.

Guideline #2: Market segment prioritization

Internal question: *Should we actively focus on all three market segments or only two?*

CAB variation: *What trends and drivers are affecting your business? With regards to the next two-to-three years, where is your business growing, what is your most important priority, and how are you planning to address it?*

Why these questions are important: There are some questions that customers cannot directly answer, such as, *which segments should we prioritize?* However, if you understand the trends and drivers affecting their growth and how they are responding, you will find clues as to which market segments are more important and more profitable for your own business.

Guideline #3: Market readiness

Internal question: *How do we ensure our products are ready for market so that customers are satisfied?*

CAB variation: *How can we deliver greater value to your company? What additional products or services would you like us* *to deliver? How effective is our marketing/sales/professional services/delivery/etc. interaction with your team?*

Why these questions are important: While the purpose of these questions is not to conduct an account review with the customers, it can be a very powerful opener for exploring opportunities that encourage these customers to think of you as a strategic partner, and not a common vendor. The objective here, of course, is to find ways to improve your relationship with these customers to increase loyalty and lifetime customer value.

Guideline #4: Competition

Internal question: *How do we balance our bookings target against competitive pressures? Must we address every move Competitor A makes, even if it detracts from other areas of our business?*

CAB variation: *Which vendors in our industry are role models? Who does a particularly good job of catering to your needs and how are they doing that?*

Why these questions are important: This is a question that must be asked with some finesse because if you ask customers directly about Competitor A, you will likely come off as being defensive and overly worried. But, if you give them an opening to compare you against alternatives, they will provide insight into which competitors or partners are more relevant to them, and which ones are not worth their time. If you listen carefully, your customers will help you define and prioritize your biggest competitive threats and partnership opportunities.

Guideline #5: Operating under resource constraints

Internal question: *Are we focused or are we doing too much?*
CAB variation: *Of the 100 things we could be doing to service*

your business, what are the top three actions/activities you think we should prioritize? If we were to do one thing to dramatically improve your business, what would you like us to do?

Why these questions are important: This is a prioritization question, and it is common to ask this type of question at the end of the CAB meeting. By then you and your team will have discussed a number of opportunities and been offered more than a few recommendations. Rather than exiting the meeting with an unprioritized list of suggestions, ask the customers to rank the options. You'll be guaranteed to leave with a clarified direction for next steps.

Common Questions to Engage CAB Customers

1. What external trends and drivers are affecting your business today? Do you expect these to change over the next three years? What are you doing to address these trends and drivers?
2. What are the growth projections for your company? How are your business priorities changing in order to address this growth?
3. Is our strategy and roadmap in line with your needs, priorities, and expectations?
4. How would you define the value we're providing to you? What kind of business partner do you consider us to be? And, how might we become a more valuable partner to you?
5. Of all the topics we've discussed, what are the top three priorities you think we should focus on?

Inferring Answers

Not all questions can be asked directly because they'll feel inappropriate or awkward. However, answers to questions like these may become clear as the conversation unfolds.

1. How do we acquire more customers like you?
2. What new markets should we invest in?
3. How can we grow revenue with these customers?
4. Should we reorganize our operations?
5. How do we perform against the competition?

4: TOP 10 LIST: WHAT YOU NEED TO KNOW ABOUT CABS

Over the past ten years customer advisory boards have become more popular, with lots of articles written about benefits, best practices, and case studies. Even so, only a small percentage of B2B companies have embraced the CAB as a tool for strategic planning and customer interaction. And of those that do, few are receiving the maximum benefit from the CAB initiative. This is because running a successful CAB requires discipline, commitment, accountability, and patience: specifically, discipline to set an objective and stay true to it throughout the entire CAB-engagement process, commitment to treat the CAB as a corporate initiative (not just an event), accountability to act on the information collected, and patience to allow the dialog with these customers to continue to grow over time.

Here are the ten most critical factors you need to know about the CAB initiative. Even as you delegate operational responsibilities to your staff, be mindful of the following. These ten simple rules of engagement will ensure the success of your CAB.

10. **Learn how to listen**. When asked to summarize how CAB discussions impacted a company's strategic direction, one CAB manager responded with the following list. "Over the years, our CAB has influenced our decision to make certain strategic acquisitions; influenced our decision *not* to make certain strategic acquisitions; drove improvements and investment in specific areas of the organization; and influenced product roadmaps and product strategy." Her company achieved success because her executives knew how and when to listen. It is human nature to fear silence. Silence feels uncomfortable, even when the stillness in the room lasts only a few seconds. But instead of giving customers time to think, some executives jump in to fill the void. They talk too much, leaving no time for customer input. Instead, let your facilitator guide the conversation. Customers should be doing 80% of the talking. This means the attending executives sit quietly and do 80% of the listening. So, take a deep breath, keep quiet, hear what your customers are saying, and focus on the implications of what they are telling you.

9. **Understand roles and responsibilities.** When it comes to executing a world-class CAB initiative, there are six key roles:

  • *Customer members:* While under a non-disclosure agreement, CAB members attend meetings with the expectation of sharing open and honest feedback in a constructive manner with your executive team. The typical length of membership is between 12 to 18 months and includes participating in one or two face-to-face meetings per year, in addition to other forms of engagement throughout the year. Membership is non-binding, meaning that there are no legal requirements nor compensation offered for their participation.

- *Executive leader* (CXO, VP, or Business Unit General Manager): While the executive leader will not be involved in the operational details of planning the CAB, he or she must maintain a visible presence and personal interest in the CAB as being a powerful asset to the company. The leader is an advocate for the CAB and looks for opportunities to rally and encourage the team doing the work. There is no substitute for attention provided by the executive leader. His or her involvement shows the importance of the CAB; without it, employees will be reluctant to engage.

- *CAB sponsor* (frequently the CMO of VP of marketing): The job of the CAB sponsor is to remove any internal obstacles that may derail the successful execution of the initiative. When internal politics get in the way, or there is a lack of cross-functional participation, the CAB sponsor steps in to align operational priorities and ensures the CAB is treated as a strategic priority and not a special project where people participate "as a favor" if and when they have the time. The CAB sponsor will also manage a dashboard of recommendations and assigned action items that result from the CAB meetings.

- *CAB manager* (may be a VP or director of marketing, product management, customer experience, or strategic *planning):* The CAB manager owns the planning and execution of the CAB meeting. As master program manager, he or she oversees everything from the selection of customers to invite, to working with content owners on the formation of the agenda, to engaging the facilitator (internal or external), to coordinating the actual CAB meeting, to documenting the meeting, and to guiding the follow-up engagement with customers. Planning a successful CAB takes an average 12 weeks of preparation, and the CAB manager drives this process.

- *Logistics coordinator (usually the events manager):* This individual is responsible for all the logistical details for any CAB meeting, including managing the contract with the meeting hall or hotel, coordinating travel with customers, developing the welcome kit, and answering any questions from customers regarding their attendance.

- *Facilitator:* The facilitator may be an internal resource or an external CAB-facilitation expert. If you choose to hire a professional CAB facilitator to guide your meeting, he or she should be involved in every step of the planning process. The professional facilitator will offer you and your content team guidance, templates, and a methodology for developing the most effective agenda, presentations, and discussion modules designed to meet your specific CAB objectives. While the role of the facilitator can be held by an internal resource, keep in mind that the art of facilitation is a skill that he or she may want to polish before the meeting. Ask if your internal facilitator would like assistance preparing for their role. This step can help them deal with nervousness, or practice engagement techniques that will not drive the discussion in a consciously- or unconsciously-biased way. Also watch out for conflicting priorities that may become distractions that will limit his or her involvement. If duties require your internal facilitator to be elsewhere and he or she can't personally commit the time required to prepare for or to be 100% certain of his or her availability to attend the CAB meeting, do your company a favor and hire a professional CAB facilitator.

8. **Treat the CAB as a top-down initiative.** The success of the CAB is directly related to the level of importance the executive leader assigns to it. If it is seen as an "activity", employees will consider a CAB as a "special project" — words guaranteed to doom the project. If the CAB is considered a "program", employees will interpret it to be a random marketing event of limited value. However, when the CAB is positioned as a "corporate initiative" it gets the cross-functional attention and participation it requires for success. While the marketing department may manage the execution, the CAB's impact will span the entire company. Said a different way, the CAB is worthless if the cross-functional executive team fails to act, allocate resources, or align and own goals in response to the information collected. The executive leader needs to hold his team accountable to listening to this customer input and incorporating it into the decision-making process. The word "initiative" gives the

CAB the proper connotation. This is a big deal and must be treated accordingly for best success.

7. **Focus on the long-term.** Increases in revenue, customer loyalty, and market share will not be achieved overnight. They take time. The *ongoing dialog* with the CAB is a tool for guidance, not immediate revenue gain. If you execute only a single CAB meeting, you will have missed the true benefits the CAB can provide. However, revenue gain will result more quickly for those companies that are in tune with their customers' businesses.

6. **Envision a successful outcome.** When executives embrace the CAB as a critical tool, the success of the CAB meeting is assured. Of course, the leadership team will have many questions, like: *Will anyone come? What will we talk about?* This is natural. Rest assured that by setting the CAB as a priority, the details will be addressed and solved to your satisfaction in time, and all CAB-related customer correspondence will reflect an attitude of energy and importance. On the other hand, when executives let their uncertainty distract them from the goal, it's hard for the team to get excited. Customers will sense the company is not yet ready, serious, or committed to the CAB. A tone of hesitancy will be unmistakable, making it easy for customers to dismiss the CAB invitation. Believe you will pull the pieces together, and you will not be disappointed. In this way, the successful execution of the CAB meeting is a self-fulfilling prophecy.

5. **Choose your questions carefully and document the answers.** When taking time to ask customers questions

and collect input, make sure this is information you are willing and able to use. It does no good to ask customers questions that you don't really care about. Nor does it help by asking questions that are vague, undirected, or where their answers are open to interpretation. Care must be taken to phrase questions in exactly the right way. If you ask unpredictable, shoot-from-the-hip questions, you will not know how to incorporate the information you collect. And be sure to document the meeting so there is a record of what was discussed. A tool of choice for many facilitators is the flipchart. While this may seem old-school in an era of modern technology, the flipchart offers a shared visual experience where everyone can see, comment on, and benefit from the notes captured. You may also have a "designated note taker" sitting at the back of the room, capturing additional details. The final documented output of the meeting should be a CAB plan-of-record — a set of notes that captures the questions asked and the answers given. It should be widely shared and referenced by all employees, not just the attending executives.

4. **Align multiple CABs under a single executive owner.** For companies that have multiple business units, it is common for each to want to run its own CAB. This makes sense if each business unit caters to a different market segment or a different set of customers. Regardless, multiple CABs need to be aligned, otherwise internal resources will be overly taxed, competing priorities will cause internal strife, and some customers may receive multiple invitations and become confused. To help synchronize multiple CAB engagements,

consider putting all CABs organizationally under one leader (sometimes referred to as a VP of customer experience). Like an air traffic controller, the job of this leader is to ensure smooth take off and landing of every CAB meeting, including the collecting, managing, and tracking of a consolidated list of CAB-generated action items and recommendations.

3. **Measure the impact.** There is nothing more powerful than a CAB sponsor armed with a dashboard that gives visibility to the recommendations and action items that result from the CAB. Without an overt way to document the opportunities and assign internal ownership, the action items will quickly be forgotten. The CAB sponsor, acting as the customer advocate, is the very best reminder to ensure the CAB remains a viable, valuable source of customer input. It ensures follow-through and momentum. And the dashboard will become incredibly important, especially when preparing for the next CAB meeting where customers expect an update on your progress since the last meeting.

2. **Communicate, communicate, communicate.** It's too easy to overlook the need to communicate internally, but sharing the output widely is required if you want this customer input and feedback to make a difference to your company. At one Fortune 500 enterprise, a CAB manager presented the findings from a CAB meeting via five different internal webinars, reaching hundreds of employees in different time zones. In each, she encouraged active, live Q&A. The webinars were also recorded and posted on a secure, internal server for easy access and archiving. Form a cross-functional VOC team

and ask them to determine what sharing mechanism works best for your employees.

And, the most important critical success factor is to always remember to:

1. **Accept that the CAB is not about you.** It's ironic but true: the agendas of the best, most eye-opening and informative CAB meetings are about your customers and how they are addressing industry trends, drivers, and priorities shaping their businesses. Of course, the host company needs to carefully select an agenda that will have relevancy to its business and product lines, but the center of the CAB universe must be the customers and their problems, not your product or service offering.

5: BRINGING YOUR CAB TO LIFE

With your CAB objectives confirmed and the executive staff aligned, you're ready for the next step. The most customer-engaging, rewarding CAB meetings follow a set of operational best-practices that keep the attention on the customer, their priorities, and the opportunities for your company to help them succeed.

To begin, assign a CAB manager to work the details. If they are unfamiliar with the inner workings of CABs and how to harness the power of this executive group, fear not. *The Flipchart Guide™ to Customer Advisory Boards, Volume 2: How to execute a world-class CAB meeting* offers an operations manual for CAB managers. It provides practical advice and a prescription for easily implementing a CAB initiative that benefits your organization and keeps your customers coming back. *Volume 2* answers questions regarding:

- Plans and timetables
- Customer selection
- The invitation process
- Venue selection
- Agenda construction
- Presentation preparation

- What to expect from the facilitator
- Information capture and dissemination
- Budget setting
- Ground rules for employees
- Frequently asked questions

You can find more information on CAB best practices, case studies, example agendas, and a variety of other relevant information on the Customer Advisory Board blog:

Your CAB resource center
http://customeradvisoryboards.wordpress.com

ABOUT THE AUTHOR

J. Michael (Mike) Gospe, Jr. is an accomplished leader, marketing strategist, and corporate executive who understands what it takes to market and sell to today's business-to-business companies. His expertise is in integrated marketing and "voice of the customer" (VOC) programs, including designing and facilitating Customer Advisory Board (CAB) meetings and executive planning sessions. Mike is co-founder and principal of KickStart Alliance (**www.kickstartall.com**), a sales and marketing leadership consulting team, where he leads the marketing operations and CAB practices. Mike also conducts team-based marketing workshops on building personas, crafting differentiating positioning statements, and drafting customer-ready messaging. His fun, practical approach and roll-up-his-sleeves attitude energizes teams, helping them get "real work done," while guiding them to the next level of marketing excellence.

Mike has authored a number of marketing- and sales-related articles, and is a frequent guest speaker at companies, marketing associations, and university business schools. His books, *Marketing Campaign Development: What executives need to know about architecting global integrated marketing campaigns* (2008), *The Marketing High Ground: The essential playbook for B2B marketing practitioners everywhere* (2011), and the new *The Marketing High Ground series* (2012) are available in paperback and for the Kindle.

Join Mike on **LinkedIn**: **www.linkedin.com/in/mikegospe**

Follow Mike on **Twitter**: **www.twitter.com/mikegospe**

OTHER WORKS

Marketing Campaign Development: What executives need to know about architecting global integrated marketing campaigns (2008) discusses the two most fundamental questions marketers are asked:

1. *How do I determine the optimum marketing communications mix?*

2. *How do I best manage internal politics to launch my marketing campaign and nurture it for best results?*

Written for marketing leaders at every level, this book answers these two key questions by taking you step-by-step through the disciplined, yet practical, process of designing truly integrated marketing communications plans that work. In these pages, you'll find a prescription for building a successful, repeatable campaign-development process, including the necessary templates and helpful, practical tips and techniques required for success. The process and best practices revealed in this book have been used at Adobe, Aspect, Cisco, Genesys, HP, Informatica, Sun, Symantec, and many other companies, large and small. You will learn the secrets for optimizing lead generation programs and achieving an even greater return on your marketing investment.

You can also find more marketing best-practices information, tips, templates, and techniques at:

http://marketingcampaigndevelopment.wordpress.com

The Marketing High Ground: The essential playbook for B2B marketing practitioners everywhere (2011) explores the following three best practices:

1. **Personas:** *how to craft a targeted persona as a reflection of a real target market*
2. **Positioning statements:** *how to draft compelling positioning statements that are truly unique when compared against competitive alternatives*
3. **Messaging:** *how to tell your story through a well-honed set of relevant messages guaranteed to engage the persona and not waste their time*

Packed with practical and powerful advice, templates, and techniques, this playbook is a valuable resource that guides marketers to dramatically improve their go-to-market programs and drive revenue. There are a lot of marketing books out there that talk a good story. This one actually shows marketers how to make a real difference. This action-oriented show-and-tell book focuses on how to build and execute more effective integrated marketing campaigns. These three best practices will put you in tune with your customers' buying process. This book shows you how, with lots of examples, descriptions, and a prescription for success. Whether you work at a large enterprise, a start-up company, or a family run business, these best practices are essential for driving successful product launches and executing integrated marketing campaigns that drive sales.

You can also find more tips, and techniques at:

http://marketinghighground.wordpress.com

26989471R00042

Made in the USA
Middletown, DE
09 December 2015